# Where Written Words Remain

## ROUTE TO MY SOUL

### JASMINE MIRÓ

# Acknowledgement

Words cannot express my deepest gratitude to my family, especially my parents, JAVS, LYNC, Noemi, Zen, my first love, Boss, and my mentor, JJP. They have all had the greatest impact on my life.

I am immensely grateful to my nephew, JM, the first person in the family to know about this book, and who, at age 5, told me "I love you best", the words that made me wish he's mine.

I could not have undertaken this journey if it were not for KPD, whose love and support for this book are unmatched, to whom I'm forever grateful for giving me and my poems a home.

I am also extremely thankful to my trusted friends who have shown me their kindness and support throughout this endeavor.

Special thanks to my dogs: Sky, Spot, and Sab, for filling my heart with gladness and love everyday.

My deepest appreciation to my inspirations: my Best Friend, my Muse, the trio of stars, my Sanctuary.

Most of all, I thank God, with whom all things are possible.

And to you, my dearest Reader, thank you for adding this book to your journey through life.

You matter to me.

# Contents

# FRAGMENTS

# Foreword

So many times, I try to make sense of everything.

And so, I write, to clear my head and quiet my heart, terrified by the flow of emotions and desperate to pause for a moment, sensing the apathy of time. I write to have a place, a space where I can let out all the thoughts and feelings that I only ever try to reconcile but can never express; the raw emotions and impulses that I try to disguise and conceal from others, even from myself, lured by the gentle nudge of delicate fear, slipping into sadness. I write as I wait in that place— as I break in the dusk and breathe in the dawn.

And in the lap of solitude, it becomes a piece. It becomes a poem.

A home.

Then there comes a sweet solace in the midst of confusion. And I feel secure and safe in my own vulnerability, this time, unmindful of the unknown, as I realize that not everything has to make sense. Not everything needs a reason, neither should it be weighed nor measured. It only needs to be felt and not fathomed. It only needs to be true.

～

*"And somewhere along the way,*
*I found the route to my soul—*
*Where written words remain."*
*~ Jasmine Miró ~*

～

# Silhouettes

# My Name

Let my feelings
       Be expressed
       In more ways
Than one.

Let my thoughts
    Be revealed
    To a stranger
    Or a loved one.

Let my heart learn
    The grace to dream
    As my mind commits
    To make it real.

Let my poetry
    Tell you who I am
    Far more than
    My name ever will.

# Fragility

In the deafening silence
    When love feels like pain
    And anger replaces affection,
There's nothing but darkness
That moves your troubled heart
To pen the truest words
Of your perfect imperfections,
To soothe your aching mind.
For in your solitude,
Darkness gives way
As it creates
A beautiful sound
And calms your storm inside.
And if you could be honest,
You know it is pain that holds you
When nobody else can.
So you learn to survive
And embrace fragility
Knowing that in the end
Hate will not prevail—
You still and will care.

# Delicate Rain

Tears
      soaked my pillow
      As the moon
Disappeared before my eyes.
My heart,
Drenched in sorrow,
But the flowers
Continued to smile,
While yesterday's
Silhouette of you
Chased the fading light.


And ever so gently,
    The yellow leaves fell
    To soothe my soul.


It's been a while—
    Since the delicate rain
    Hugged the night.

# Blue

Isn't it beautiful?
   Serenity
   In two kinds of blue
When the sky meets the sea
And I dream
Of you and me,
When the blue
Touches another blue,
Do they become
Like me without you?


Under the golden sun
   The sky and the sea,
   They kiss,
   Pure bliss that I miss,
   For you are not here with me,
   So near yet so far
   Like the most luminous star.
   And so, I remain bluer than blue
   Each moment that I am without you.

# Coffee, Please

Words still delight me
        In my sleep
        Like free flowing coffee
        In my dream,
And as I wake up
To weave,
It usually ends
With a weird twist,
Possibly something like this,
Or just anything
That would make me think
Whether it's quite melancholic
Or sightly dramatic,
Perhaps a bit romantic.


My words
        May not make you happy,
        But it's fine with me
        Because I write them
        For me.

# Sit Beside Me

S it beside me
　　　　So happy thoughts
　　　　Of pretty things
Will rhyme
And I may write you
Into a poem.

Come here
　　　And inspire me
　　　So you will see
　　　How words will overflow,
　　　Then you will know.

Sit next to me
　　　So I may hide you
　　　In my poetry
　　　And make you
　　　Immortal
　　　And my all.

# Questions

If I would come to you
    And tell you that I need you,
        Would you hold me in your arms,
And comfort me with a kiss?


If I tell you how I feel
    Would you believe it for real?
    Will you be with me tonight
    And tell me that everything's all right?


If I tell you that I love you
    That, without you, I'll be blue
    Would you choose to stay and see
    Or would you walk away from me?


If only these words would be enough
    To let you know that it's true
    Then these words won't remain questions,
    Questions I cannot ask of you.

## Pretty Things

The gentleness of his touch thrilled her
Her soul, quite mesmerized
As the windows opened for them
And the ocean met the night,
Melting away
The purest of blackness in her eyes,
Slowly appeasing
Her gloom, doubts and frights
By the warmth of his embrace,
Graced with a dancing flicker of light.

It puzzles her
How they fit into each other,
A delicate comfort
Filling the most intimate of needs;
Petals unfold, as she sees
Through veiled eyes— his glowing soul,
Feelings untold, yet
There's no need for spoken words
To illuminate
the wondering desires that followed.

. . .

She breathes him in
 With the greatest of ease,
 Unwrapping his sacred scars
 And deepest secrets,
 Exhaling the bittersweet memories
 To live in the moment,
 And let go of her fate
 That was much worse than death;
 Only trusting his hand that saved her
 From breaking her own heart.


Her heart, now beats fast with delight,
 It seems sweeter than forever,
 His kiss deepens and neither their past
 Nor their future linger;
 The dawn cannot be that far
 As the moon bids farewell,
 And his loving eyes cut through
 All illusions and spells,
 For time revealed to them
 What nothing else could tell.


A sudden gust of wind and his touch
 Sent shivers down her spine,
 Every word she could not say,
 In silent phrases they remain
 As intense, sweet sensations
 Of scattered hints infiltrating through;
 He opened her with care
 And the subtle hues of emotions felt so true;
 Two silhouettes becoming one,
 Created the perfect view.

In the garden of stars
    Reflecting rainbow tints of lovely dreams,
    Surrounded by little yellow flowers
    And his heart that sings.
    He smiled at her
    As if she's the only one that matters,
    Though unsure how to go back to the start:
    She spreads her wings.
    And as the world sleeps,
    They, too, dream of pretty things.

# Dreams

You touched her
    In ways she yields
        To every longing,
Every desire;
Dreams fulfilled,
As stars are felt
In each caress
And tender smile.

# Your Name

The skies are bleeding
As I cut my heart open,
Your name,
Beautifully engraved,
Unspoken;
Chasing silhouettes
That never quite leave,
I write without regrets,
And self-destruct in poetry
Of consecrated heartaches.

# If I Could

I would freeze
    Time with you
    If I could,
For who am I now
Without time,
Without you?
Just a little longer,
I would if I could,
Because time—
I need it as you.

# When Silence Speaks

I give in.

You're a drug to let me feel
    The sweetest of needs
    To be still
    In your kiss;
    Your eyes love me
    As the soft scarf
    Neatly fell on the floor,
    And I whisper words
    Of how I want
    To be devoured.

We hold on to the night;
    When silence speaks,
    I let you touch me—

To be one with my soul.

# *Surrender*

I surrender.

I breathe you in,
  And adore
  The taste of your love on my skin,
  Sweet, intoxicating,
  Tenderly cherished, uncontrolled emotion
  Penetrating through;
  With every fiber of my being,
  I'm craving you.

I surrender.

As you claim my soul,
  Tears fall.

I, then, know I belong to you.

## Your Love

L et your heart go back
    To a minute that's gone,
    A moment once cherished
And turned into a poem.
Let falling petals nestle safe
In the soft arms of a song,
Until the waves of sadness fade
Into rhyming lines that belong.
Let the waning moonlight
And loneliness wash ashore
In glittered reflections
Of subtle gray and deep gold.
And in our separate space,
Please listen through silence
As the coming of summer,
Once again, warms your soul:
Please remember how it felt
To be loved just the same,
Remember how tenderly
I whispered your name,

And know that I think of you—
    I wish you love
    Like the one you gave me,
    A love that lingers on
    In me and my poetry.

# Memories of Stars

Take these words
       And hold them close,
       For when your heart
Feels tired and cursed;
Take all my thoughts
As midnight spells
Soften and blur
The memories of stars,
Unscripted, unrehearsed.
Though the flower
Holds back
Her love for the moon,
You're ingrained within,
Because always
Is never too soon.

# Your Truth

Will you ever know
 The secret poets keep?
 Will they ever show
 How they truly love so deep?
A soul's heart
Will not reveal so much,
As you must know the art
To feel things
Unseen, untouched,
For there's beauty in pain
And in the secrets
Of your youth,
Memories stain
When loneliness
Becomes your truth.

# Route to My Soul

Would you care?
    Would you even dare
    To go to this place,
    And let your soul dance
As you freeze in the sun
And you burn in the rain?


This is the road
    Where you will never want
    To walk alone,
    The path that leads
    To my playground unknown,
    My favorite hideout
    With an endless pouring rain,
    My secret garden
    Where I hide my tears,
    Drown my sorrow,
    Bury my pain.

So go in peace
    And just let me be
    As I scream in silence.


Don't you ever dare
    To come near this place
    Unless you know how to listen
    To what I'm not saying,
    And read with your heart,
    The words
    I never dared to speak.

# Moon Girl

Sometimes she's weird,
 Sometimes she's strange,
  Often, she's brutally honest,
But, most times, she's sweet
And just as scared as you.
Still, with all her heart
And with all her soul,
She truly loves
And expects nothing in return.

# By Heart

When your soul
          Is aching to speak,
        It seeks its equal—
      Someone
Who understands by heart
What the mind
Cannot,
At all,
Comprehend.

# When Time Stands Still

How clever pain is
    That it renders you speechless,
    For it doesn't heal all wounds
    And bruises.
So do not medicate at all,
This deep cut
That's tearing your soul.
Just let it bleed profusely
As your heart weeps
Until it bleeds
No more
In serenity's kiss.
And you find you
In those blank pages
As you lovingly give in to
The seemingly
Sweet emptiness,
When your mind
So chooses
To be lonely,

And soothingly embraces
    The unspoken
    Words of insanity—
    When time stands still
    Against its will.

# Silent Heart

A voice she hears...
        Was she dreaming
            In the midst of longing?
She started to listen
To what's unseen,
A melody echoing
To the core of her being,
The once untamed heart
Now, calmly beating.
The gray skies cleared,
Traces of profound sorrow
No longer exist,
Only a spell she couldn't resist,
When their lips met
And their souls touched
As his love engulfed
Her silent heart.

# Still Falling

❧

Some days, life feels light,
    Most days, it just does not.
    Some days, I love the healing sun,
But most days, I wish for rain so I can dance
And let my worries fade like embers
And maybe then you'd stay for a little longer.
Some days, I still hear you singing,
Most days, just my heart, breaking.
And these days, silence has become my only language
To appease my dark thoughts and deep anguish,
A lie so painstakingly crafted
To soothe the words better left unsaid.
Even though this lost road
Is hurting,
And I lose track of time,
You'll find me here—
Still falling.

# Sunshine in My Soul

L ost in a maze,
      I once wandered
      Hopelessly
In the rain.

But now,
    I finally know
    Where the sun
    Shines from.

And it's from deep
    Within my soul.

Summer has not ended.

It is here to stay
    As long as
    There is
    A jasmine left
    To feel the sun.


I free my mind,
    Open my heart,
    And feel it, too.


I feel its warmth
    And feel blessed.


I am blessed.


I have found myself
    And I don't want to forget;
    I will not forget
    That I define me.

# *The Heart*

The heart never measures what it feels;
It only knows what it loves
Even when it breaks,
As hope whispers sacred words
Defying reasons
And organized chaos.

# If You Only Knew

If you only knew,
  You will never question why,
  For my eyes speak but a few,
Through silent cries, I try
And let my heart write
What my lips deny.

# Fragments

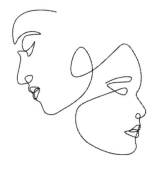

# Softer than Love

There is a kind of love,
     Between two people,
     That never fades away,
Regardless of their choices—
No matter the pain.

So I pray,

If loving you breaks my heart,
     Then let pain be softer than love.

# Fragments

S omewhere
   In some of these pages,
   You will find
Snippets of you,
And as you read
The words
Better left unsaid;
You will see
How I hide you
In my poetry.


Sometimes
   In some of these thoughts,
   You will find
Bittersweet things
And it will hurt
Or cause a smile,
But it's all right,
As you will know
How you made me feel
And bleed.

And somewhere,
 In some of these pictures
 You will find
 Fragments of you,
 My first love,
 For you
 Have always been
 My favorite subject,
 Never myself,
 Just you.

# Words

I wear the words
　　To shield me
　　From breaking,
And as the quiet night
Gives in to despair—
I gently let go.

# Illuminate

May goodbye
    Be kinder than hello,
        As pain illuminates
Forgiveness
When hearts
Find no words.

# Once More

Today
   I saw you cry,
   Without words
I hugged you close.

All of a sudden
   I was a willing soul
   And once again
   I see you beautiful.

To be lost in you
   Is like walking into fire,
   As I breathe you in
   It feels like loving a knife.

# The Shore

My eyes will always
Search for yours,
Let this be a blessing
Or a curse,
And even though
My mind tells me no,
My heart
Still wishes for you.

And so my soul will always find you
Like the ocean finds its shore,
And even if it hurts like hell,
I will find bliss
In the deepest blue
And darkest pain.

# Only Love

Sometimes,
There is a silent raging,
A wounded child in us
That needs to heal,
Not by time,
But by love that could hold
The soul to be still—
Only love.

# Heaven-Sent

And if, in tears
And bittersweet memories,
I'd still believe
You're heaven-sent,
Let me love you,
Honestly
And always,
To my heart's content.

# *Forever Changed*

Beneath the trees
    And stars that grieve,
    I write this piece
In bluest ink,
Lost to the tales
And sadness of the twilight,
Courageously reminiscing
How summer died in your eyes
Under the misty skies
While the hues of December
Nurtured the frozen tears
Of the embers.

And I think of us,
    Of what could have been,
    But with no bitterness,
    Without regrets,
    As I have seen
    The jasmines smiled
    This time last year.

And though I cried, I loved;
 I welcomed
 The winter in my heart,
 For you loved me, too,
 And I was forever changed.

# As Flowers Ache

My heart still remembers
Time and again
As flowers ache
To smell the scent of rain,
How it never ends—
And never will.

# Dream Away

Will it be my turn?
   To stand
   Next to you,
   Maybe someday.
For now,
I'll dream away.

# *How*

How do I let go
   Of something
   So beautiful?

How can I not love
   With all my heart
   And soul?

How can I leave
   If there's no anger
   Or regret?

How do I move on
   When you asked me
   To never forget?

# There Is Love

Goodbye
    Doesn't mean gone;
      The sun only hides
Behind dark drapes drawn
By the harsh hands of time
While the moon waits
To share the dawn,
Admiring crackled quartz
On midnight sands.
Though unseen
And without words,
The stars still breathe
Your light, faultless
In their eyes,
For in the sweetest
Lips of silence,
There is love.
And still—
It's more than enough.

# Perfection

L etting you go is self-deception
      That has become the hardest part
      In my quest for perfection,
It has cost me my heart.
To try to live a life of excellence,
My love, I would have to abandon,
But what is the meaning of happiness
If reality is, in truth, an illusion?


So let my heart break a little further
      As my mind gives the final verdict.
      Let me lie to myself once more
Just to keep me safe from all the hurt.
Let me not suffer yet again
In loving and then leaving you.
Let me not feel the unavoidable pain
And the consequence of losing you.

But if by chance we meet again
    And you'd ask me to be true,
    Would you be able to discern
    If in all honesty, I'd answer you?
    Without the need to introspect,
    I'd tell you this and not deny:
    "It's never worth it to be perfect
    In everyone's eyes but mine,
    It never was, and it never will,
    For without you I'm only half as real,
    When deep inside, deep in my soul—
    You're the perfection that I know."

# Forgotten Forever

There's chaos in stillness
When the heart remembers
Love's forgotten forever.

# For a While

I'll stay in my dreams for a while,
Where loving you does not hurt,
And we never said goodbye.

# Empty Space

The day
Starts to fade
And the sun
Begins to set,
We drift apart
With sad hearts
And sadder eyes
As our secrets sleep
While in dreams
We weep,
For every tight hug
And soft kisses,
For pillow moments
And shared stories—
I will remember.
And until then,
All of that space,
Without you in it,
Is empty.

# One Day Soon

Let me wait
While the stars
Echo loneliness
In between our hearts;
Let me hold on to someday,
For today, it's too late,
No matter
How much I wish
To hug you closer,
I can no longer
Dry your eyes
Each time
You feel empty inside.
But please
Don't forget me
As I'll love you again
And I'll love you better
One day soon—
Once more.

## If Only

Cut the losses
         Before things get worse,
         Just risk what
You're willing to lose.


How I hope
      The same thing goes
      For when the heart
      Is slightly bruised,
      Prevent the bleeding
      Before bruises
      Turn to wounds
      Ever so deep
      That even
      The very soul hurts.


Cut the losses
      And reduce the loss,
      Don't risk what
      You can't afford to lose.

If only this is an option
    We could choose
    For when our hearts
    Break in two,
    And in desperation
    Our plans fall through,
    To learn this art
    And find reasons
    To save what's left
    Of our pained souls.


Cut your losses,
    Don't be left
    Holding the bag
    For far too long.

# Broken

I will run away,
       For to hold you once again
       Will leave me broken.

## Healing

**H**ealing is elusive when love
Hides behind unsaid words—
Wounding more.

# It Didn't Rain that Day

⚬⚬⚬

It didn't rain that day
    To wash my cares away,
    But there were raindrops falling
While the music, still playing,
And it felt good to just let it flow
As wandering thoughts follow.


A blast from the past,
    How long will it last?
    My heart did wonder
    As these thoughts outnumber,
    Things that I've been missing
    I, then, keep remembering.


Scattered musings,
    Swirling feelings,
    Now I'm beginning to feel
    That I can never will
    Escape these silent sighs
    That reverberate in my mind.

# I'll Remember

L et warm raindrops fall,
     Though time blurs the memories,
     It doesn't stop the rain.


Let the pain remain
     As time just softens the storm,
     Fate's still bleeding words.


In silence, we yearn
     For time never heals all wounds,
     But I'll smile through tears.


And I'll remember
     Loving you without regrets
     As I chase the sun.


Made of broken parts,
     My soul still embraces yours
     In my heart of hearts.

# Dear Heart

Please teach me, dear heart,
    To dance through uncertainties
    When I get cold feet.

# Smile

Underneath the mask
    Of her stifled emotions,
  She smiled with her eyes.

# Hurt You

I want to hurt you
For the million ways
You broke
My heart
In million pieces,
But I won't,
For I couldn't
Because I love you.

# Love's Sad Melody

This wanderlust
    Tore us apart
       When dreams faded
Like morning mist,
But we'll heal
As pain turns to
A distant memory
Of love's sad melody.

# Your Reality

You start recognizing
  That you're still breathing
  Because your heart still breaks,
While you're dead awake.

You woke up from a dream
  And nothing was as it seemed,
  Everything was only a polaroid
  Of spaces and places,
  A glimpse of time,
  Fleeting moments of bliss
  And nothing more.

You realize that
  It's just an imagination,
  A vision you tried
  So hard to create,
  To break free
  From that feeling
  Of not feeling at all,

To convince yourself
That you are the host
Of your own party,
And that you can do
All that you desire
Because it is your story.


It is your reason,
    Your excuse to be stubborn,
    To be silly,
    To be crazy,
    To be wild,
    To feel alive,
    Because you dread
    That you're just about
    To fade out,
    Not knowing what to do
    To keep living,
    To keep breathing,
    Because you're slowly
    Giving up.


So then again you try
    To close your eyes,
    Because you finally realized
    That you'd rather drift
    Into a deep sleep
    Of gentle surrender
    For a little longer
    Than be awake
    With a thousand
    Troubling thoughts
    And invisible tears.

                        .   .   .

To be lost in this story
    Is your only reality—
    All else is folly.

# Beyond Words

I fell in love with you
       Long before
            I had the courage
To admit it to myself.


But let silence
       Keep this deepest secret
       As my stubborn heart
       Misses you—


Beyond words


And always.

# Silence

Please listen closely
    To what I am not saying—
    Hear my heart's silence.

## Grace

L ike the gentle rain,
    Your words soothe with sweet embrace,
    Subtlety of grace.

# The Best of Me

I love you
>Because of the sweet little things
>That you say or do,
>The little big moments with you,
>They mean the world to me,
>All else fades away.

I love you
>Because you are the voice
>Aligning my thoughts
>When I couldn't find the words,
>The solace I long to feel
>When the world is cruel.

You are the melody,
>The music and the lyrics
>Meant to be sung;
>You are my song.

I love you
    Because of who you are,
    Even the way you hide your pain
    When you look away,
    And the way you smile
    With sadness in your eyes.


In you,
    I found a reason,
    The heart that I lack
    When I couldn't feel anything,
    When life had no meaning
    And I stopped believing.


I love you
    Because of all these amazing things
    That you say or do,
    Inspiring me
    To do my best
    And give the best of me.


Words will never be enough,
    But if one day you'd ask,
    "Why do I love you?"
    I will tell you this and so much more:


For I know I love you
    Because of infinite reasons
    My mind
    Cannot explain,
    But my soul
    Always knew.

# *Unconditional Love*

Sometimes
    Unconditional love
    Means goodbye,
And letting go
Of what makes
You and me bleed.

# What Matters

It doesn't matter
If it already ended.
All that matters
Is that it happened,
That it was real,
That you, once, loved me.

# If You Ever Need Me

Why do we always see
  The same side of the moon?
  What makes the clock tick
  And how does it keep time?
How did we click
When we're the complete opposite?
Can this be explained
By mysterious entanglement?

Despite our big differences
  And a few similarities,
  We write our sentences
  Of infinite possibilities,
  We connected in a heartbeat
  As we fit together
  Like puzzle pieces,
  Interlock with one another.

The sun will continue to rise
    With its brilliant light
    On both sides
    Of your sky and mine,
    The moon will be
    illuminated to shine bright
    And we will always
    See the same side.


The clock will keep time,
    So accurate and precise,
    Even when our thoughts give in
    And doubts overtake,
    But regardless of time,
    Circumstance, or place,
    The invisible string
    That ties us will never break.


While we try to live
    Our lives to the full,
    We are met by our dreams
    To carry us through
    For what we have
    Is crazy beautiful,
    You feel like home,
    I feel safest with you.

Albeit from afar, you enrich my life
    In countless ways,
    And as you stand where the sand
    Meets the blue sea,
    Even in the darkest hour
    Before a new day—
    I will be here
    If you ever need me.

# Stories

# Amid the Chaos

I see more
    Through your eyes,
    So much more
Than you realize,
For they betray your lies
Despite your endless tries
And elaborate disguise.
I see more
Amid the chaos,
Through the windows
To your soul,
Behind fake smiles
And inner sobs,
When pain intensifies
As your heart screams
What your mind denies.

# Strawberries

S trawberries,
     You never liked those, but I do.
     You prefer hot chocolate
Over coffee,
But sometimes
You drink espresso, too, with me.


You love to ride
     The mountain bike,
     I never learned how to,
     But in your competition,
     I have always cheered for you.
     You listen to metal and grunge
     While I listen to Einaudi's Nuvole Bianche.

You love the nightlife
    With your friends,
    I love to write and I don't mind
    To wait for you all night
    And until dawn.


We did hike together
    To the top of the mountain,
    Spent the night in a tent
    To see the sea of clouds.
    I got sick the next morning,
    My fragile body
    Couldn't stand the cold.


I could go on and on
    With this list of things
    That we don't share in common
    But the bottom line
    Will always be this—
    Despite never having learned
    To love the things you love,
    And despite everyone else
    Telling me not to,
    I did learn to love you.

# Always

I don't crave heartbreak
   To start anew;
   I never thought I'd write again,
For without my muse I won't have a clue.
You smiled as you tried to shed light
On the opposite of what's true;
You believed I'll only ever go to pen more,
When joy aches for sorrow.


Lost in a daydream, you went to war for me,
   And so did I, for you,
   But with each passing day,
   Holding on demanded more than letting go.
We wear pain like a crown,
But are dreams enough to see us through?
I longed to hold the moon,
But fate left me behind when it befriended you.
So like prayers lost among the stars,
We let go, though we never wanted to.

And death was a day when we walked away,
    When we finally let go,
    But don't grieve for me, for I continued
    To pen the echoes of summer for you.
    In an absence that pains, I wonder,
    Do you write about sad blooms, too?
    And if so, as you write, do you remember
    Loving me when you're blue?


"The moon is beautiful, isn't it?",
    I want to tell you that, too,
    Each time that my heart and my soul
    Form the words inspired by you.
    But even in one frozen moment,
    I'd close my eyes rather than look at you,
    For I dare not say a word or meet your gaze,
    But I still think of you:
    I saved a little hope and space,
    Always, reserved for only you.

# No Matter the Pain

Does the moon mourn
      When a flower dies?


Deep in the forest,
      In the dead of night,
      Though a thin sheet of ice
      Upon her casket folds
      In all the shadowed corners,
      And sad memories shimmer
      And fade—
      It blooms again
      In death's secret garden.


So don't fret.
      Hold on and stay.
      Don't look away
      When you see her frail.

It matters not
    When darkness bleeds
    Rueful reflections
    Upon her crystal wings;
    Despite dripping pain,
    She still waits
    For when the wolf moon
    Whispers your name.


Time neither stops for us,
    Nor does it heal all wounds,
    But love transcends time:
    It knows no bounds.


And so she waits,
    For May to bloom
    As she breathes for love
    Once more.


For everything changed
    When you loved her;
    She'll love you—
    No matter the pain.

# In Your Garden

Will you ever really see me?
          Delicate if you remember,
          Easily flawed,
          But the missing petal
     Of my imperfection
     Might just grab
     Your attention.


Even though I know
          There can never
          Be only one flower
          In your garden,
          Please make me your star.


I hope that If you
          Ever will come to me,
          Please touch me
          Like no other can.

I will wait for you
     From sunrise to sunset
     To capture me at my best
     Like I was worth the wait,
     The only one that matters,
     For the way you'll look at me
     Will set me apart from the rest.


So please come to the garden
     While I still breathe
     for your smile,
     And you will always find me—
     Waiting here.

# Her Eyes

She once wandered
    Aimlessly through the dark streets
    Of the coldest hearts,
Drenched in her pain,
Lost in a tale of lovers and friends.
And you found her,
Silence has ended
And the passion has begun.


When the music played,
    You both danced in the rain.
    You held her tightly that night
    Until the morning came.
    And she moved you,
    Every part of you,
    Seeing right through you,
    Stirring up the corners of your mind,
    Sinking deep into your veins,
    Embracing the depths of your soul,
    Taking your heart by surprise,
    Leaving you breathless, but satisfied.

And when you stared
    Deeply into her eyes,
    You knew you will never
    Ever want to say goodbye.

# Stalemate

W ill you ever know?
      Not so long ago,
   I fell in love with you,
   But chose to let you go.

No one sets out to lose
   Battles we are told to wisely choose:
   To win, I'd give up all my pieces as a sacrifice,
   But what is winning, if even love won't suffice?

In the battle of the minds
   With two timers built in one clock,
   Would you rather willingly resign,
   Lose by timeout, or end in a deadlock?

I'd move the king to safety
    And likely win in blitz and nine-sixty,
    Yet I'd be lost, with only myself to blame,
    For, without you, I will never be the same.


Such a losing game to fall,
    But to be stalemated in a painful way
    Where neither side can win or lose, and risk it all—
    Who dares to say?

## In Your Eyes

I whispered words
        To the wind
        To make you feel me
Under your cold winter rising sun,
As you lay still,
Sleeping peacefully,
It started raining in my heart.
Smoke memories
Funneled into the abyss
Of fears and analogies
When conviction
Betrayed the truth
As the mind denied what's real
For it spoke not of affection,
But of rational direction
While silence consoled pain
And we held on to remain sane.

But know
>That I yearn for you,
>Never a day that I never will,
>Despite despair
>Disguised as happiness
>Behind saccharine coated smiles
>Clouded by deep sadness;
>And as hope waves goodbye,
>Can you feel my tears in your eyes?

# *Interlude*

If death is just an interlude,
    Then it must be wonderful
    To be buried in this breathing space
Between passages and verses
In a strangely familiar melancholy,
It must be quite lovely,
To be drowned in everything
That we've never been,
And cease to exist
In all those what could have been,
Between the here and now
That wasn't meant to be,
Such sweet demise
in momentary nothingness,
Holding on, but no longer stuck
In between fantasy and reality
While mistrusting my sanity
In a bell jar of starlight and dreams
As red turns to pearls
Of monstrous despair;
Just longing yet no longer fighting
To death, not anymore,

Just aching
    To die only to breathe again,
    To live again.


If death is just an interlude,
    Then, it will not be the last time,
    I will find you again somehow,
    And I would gladly let you in
    To the door of my heart,
    To the route of my soul.
    In another life, I will meet you there;
    I will be there—
    To love you once more,
    And let our own story begin again.


So if death is just an interlude,
    Oh, dear death,
    Will you be my friend?

# If Tomorrow Never Comes

I once asked death to be my friend,
     But wicked fate betrayed her instead.


If stars were gods, would they decide
     What's wrong and what's right?
     To love or not to love,
     Either way, we would have tried,
     Crushing the heart of the flower
     As they threw the first stone
     When the only thing it knew
     Was to adore the moon.


While they were trying to stay
     With reasons to leave, time laughed,
     As they wrote a thousand letters
     That still may never be enough,
     And though your past and mine
     Never turned the skies to gray,
     The vestiges of burnt sienna stained
     The present that seemed so far away.

So she waits, for the morrow
    Of new chapters, though uncertain,
    For in the next day, she knows
    She can bear to burn in the rain;
    You might find her in that place
    Where nothing else matters,
    A space where her smile
    For you never falters.


But perhaps, all these will remain
    Nothing but a silent scream,
    For the petals will soon wilt
    On torn out pages of a dream,
    If the sun rises no more,
    If tomorrow never comes,
    And we're just left to mourn
    For the death of a million moons.


I did ask death to be my friend,
    I guess fate would not, at all,
    Betray her in the end.

# Softened Sunrises and Wounded Spaces

I miss you today,
    And I ache:
        Maybe jasmines, too,
Have thorns
That silently break
Its little flower's petal,
For I, too, hurt
As my heart
Still sings your song,
Albeit from afar,
The stars
Felt the same
When your name
Left a sweet scar.

And while the moon
    Finds the sun
    Beleaguered by
    Hope-covered regret,
    I take comfort
    From softened sunrises
    And wounded spaces
    As I rhyme and wonder.


What if love was a rose
    Without thorns,
    Would it be less painful
    When it doesn't
    Bleed words
    For the soul?
    Wouldn't it be easier
    To rewrite our story
    In azure skies,
    With sun-kissed marigolds
    Between our poems
    And love in our eyes?


Maybe then,
    We will only hold
    Each other,
    And nothing else
    Would ever matter.

# Valentine's Day

There was a time
 In my life
 When I asked God why—
Why love feels like pain
When they say
That it's from Him?
I asked God why
He allowed me to feel
The most excruciating
Of all pain,
And as my silent prayer
Turned to bitter tears,
Dripping pain
Cascading without end
Down my face
And into my veins,
My broken wings
Felt only weakness
Until pain seduces
And convinces
The moon
And me to be alone.

You took your last breath
    Right after Valentine's Day;
    Since you've been gone,
    Love feels nothing but pain.

# Forever Lonely

I feel you near
        As grief solidifies,
        And fireflies dance
To the silent cries
Of my breaking heart,
Questioning my mind,
"How do I start?",
But don't be sorry
When you see me hurting,
Just leave the arms
Of the heavens
And come back, please,
As there's no other way
For the rain to go away,
This deep despondency
Pierced my reverie.

So here I am again
    Trying to write,
    Trying to make sense
    Of this tragedy;
    Here I am still,
    Reliving your memories
    In a field of melancholy.


I guess I'll never be ready
    For without you now,
    Even the flowers
    Will forever be lonely.

# All My Tears

I used to fear
> The empty space
> Inside of me.

I sometimes hear
> The daunting stillness
> I cannot see.

I still shoulder
> The burden of flawed choices,
> And it's never easy.

Now in great danger,
> Children, in their innocence,
> Perished unjustly.

Their selfless mothers,
> Not leaving their cold bodies,
> Chose the same destiny.

.  .  .

Their helpless fathers
        Mourned in raging silence
        At the sight of this cruelty.


What's worse than this nightmare?
        Streets run red as angels
        Breathe their last in misery.


All my tears
        Are nothing, not even close,
        Compared to their agony.

# Lying Eyes

What would these eyes see
        If these were the last
        Falling leaves that tell a story?
    Where do we go?
How do we start?
How do I carry on
With these empty pages
Of my heart?
How do we read
Between the lines,
With the distance
That we drew between us?
How do we let go
Of the letters we never read
With the words
That weren't meant
To be left unsaid?

I tried to look at you
    With lying eyes,
    And hoped that
    You won't recognize
    The deepest love
    I have inside.


As I blinked at the streak
    Of clouds fading away,
    You looked at me
    And I silently wished
    There's another way.


You told me
    I'm the one that got away.
    The truth is:
    I never really left,
    For I've always wanted
    To stay.
    I closed my eyes,
    Trying to shut my mind off,
    Wondering when
    My heart would say,
    "I've had enough".
    But I know
    I never will stop,
    For you are my one great love;
    I still care even to this day
    And my eyes
    Cannot really lie—
    So I looked away.

## 11:11

We danced through the colors
Of each ethereal night,
We listened to the heartbeats
Of the breathing galaxy;
We deserved to dream
Until we saw
The lovely moon cried
When time unfolded
The forgotten names
Of cold blooms
In misery.


And as the heart
Waged a constant war
Against the mind, dead awake,
We suffered slowly;
I couldn't stay away,
But the sun in my eyes
Refused to shine,
And the poet in agony
Gently let go
Of me.

What remains
  When hope
  Is our weapon
  That made us bleed?
  These are the lasting,
  Sacred scars
  It carved on me.
  Defying my reasons,
  My very shield,
  I left the battlefield
  Of painful mystery.


But my love, look up,
  Up ahead
  Regardless of our choices
  And our history—
  And always,
  Remember the wind
  With these unspoken words,
  Written for an eternity.

# An Open Letter to My Soulmate

T his is one of those times when I'd sit in this little corner of my room, with a smile on my face and in my heart as I write to you.

And I picture you under the magical aurora sky, in your corner of the world, gazing at the stars.

It's so often thought that there's only one soul out there for each of us. I wondered if you're that one soul in the entire universe that's meant for me to love forever regardless of time, circumstance, or place.

What sets you apart from the rest? Are you the string of my fate? I used to think that meeting you was purely by chance, but does coincidence exist in fate, even for once?

As our story unfolded, for the wildest mystery I know, we danced with a profound sense of familiarity, of home. The once blank pages, devoid of purpose, finally kissed our pens' truest emotions. And as time went on, something in me has changed as if the stars moved themselves and rearranged. With you, I feel alive, for the first time, for the last; without you, I fall apart.

It matters not why, how or when, all I know is that I've learned to embrace the entirety of your being. I live each day knowing you're there; holding moonlight, smiling, sharing the dark, touching me in ways my soul recognizes yours, with or without words. I did wish that we met where timing was neither an issue nor a question. Nevertheless, I know that loving you is something I have no control over. It just happened.

You came along. And ever so gently, you held my soul.

Perhaps in rare aurora skies and deep city lights,
    in a recollection of things yet unseen,
    in another set of stories yet untold,
    in rhyming lines yet unspoken,
    I'd hold on, remembering...
    while the stars and my dreams collide
    until my words find you.

I won't tell you to stay. I just need to tell you goodnight.
    And I miss you.
    And that, without a doubt, I love you.

## Don't Leave

It's beautiful. To know that there's one soul who understands the deepest part of you. Without even having to explain yourself.

You just feel that connection with them so strong you never want them to ever leave. Regardless of what they are or who they are, wherever they may be.

They might fly away one day, but somewhere in your heart, you just want them to stay. And hold them close in that special part of you that you have reserved almost only for yourself. But somehow you allowed them to see you, how you really are, how you think and most of all, how you feel. That somehow, you fear losing them, so you ask and you tell them not to leave.

Without reason, without explanation.
    Just two words.

Don't leave.

# I Miss You

The hardest part of letting go is not fearing for love to fade from the hearts of two; It is knowing that both of you still love each other, but not having enough courage to fight to be together. Because the hardest part of love is the things that we have to give up.

I know there's nothing behind me but lost stars and memories, yet you're with me wherever I go. I can't take away all your pain, so in silence, I remain, while my heart screams all over again, echoing in my mind, nothing but your name. Every. Single. Time. Always. And I don't want to look at you because your eyes tell me the truth.

I'm not trying to write a poem. I'm not trying to be poetic because, right now, I can't make the words to rhyme. But let me write to reconcile my head with my mind. Let me be honest with myself even just for today as the dawn breaks. Because always is longer than forever.

And I miss you. So. Damn. Much.

## Before Sunrise

I always thought I loved sunsets.
   And then one day,
      I woke up to the sound of the waves.
   Half asleep, I walked down the beach
   And I saw it:
   A magical moment before sunrise.


And I thought of you... of us.
   I close my eyes to find you here with me.


The taste of you lingers in my soul,
   As I take you in, I become whole,
   Your lips whispered my name,
   I held on to you; no, this isn't a game—
   For I've never been the same.

# While the Stars Fall Asleep

❧

The moon reflects the sun's light
    As clouds disappear in delight
    And while the stars fall asleep,
Dreaming of finding a heart to keep,
My mind is wide awake,
Drawn into the colors of daybreak.


Is it too early to take my heart back?
    Is it unfair to care that I lack
    The courage to speak up?
    Will it ever stop?


Will it be enough?
    Maybe just give up,
    For there's more to it than love.

# My Light

You are light
        In the dark,
        You burn
To linger,
You bleed
To feel,
You reflect
Your truth.


And you love,
        You just love
        Without reason,
        Without excuse.
        You shine,
        Then you fade,
        And you die
        A little each time.
        Yet in me,
        You live
        Forever
        And a day.

# New Love

What would you say to someone
Who has promised you a life together,
Forever there, until the very end,
But left you way before it even started?
Would you dare ask if it meant different
Compared to what you believe in?

Would you explain why "I love you" is sacred
Especially when, with a promise, it is paired?
Would you even want to know if he, too, cried
Like the way you did when he said goodbye?
Did he know how you dreaded being alone,
And you wished he'd stay for one moment more?

Would you be ready to face tomorrow,
Despite your deep, lingering sorrow,
And let go, for you can't unbreak what's broken?
Would you forgive and forget without disdain?
Would you let time heal, would you love again,
Release the pain to allow a new love to begin?

# The Panda and the Orca

L et me tell you a story
In pure simplicity,
This is not scary,
Later you will see,
It's just something
That makes me happy.

And the story goes this way...

Once upon a time...
There's no damsel in distress
Or a sleeping princess,
Trapped in a magical castle
To be rescued by her prince.

I just wasn't sleepy yet, so I wrote this.

Here it goes.

There's a panda who loves an orca,
But this orca is not really reckless,
Just a plain pain in the neck
That always doubts and asks.

"I love you",
Said the panda
To the orca
One starry night.

The orca cringed in disbelief
And tried hard
Not to be sarcastic,
"Though I'm a panda of the sea
I don't eat a bamboo tree."

"I still love you, anyway,
And bamboo is not a tree",
Said the panda to the orca
That same starry night
While giggling in delight.

The orca further replied,
A bit teary-eyed,
"I am a killer whale
In everyone's eyes,
Don't you fear for your life?"

The panda smiled winsomely
And blew kisses to the orca
While the sky created
A beautiful aurora,

"No, I don't fear for my life,
        You're not a killer whale
        In my eyes,
        You are just
        Misunderstood oftentimes,
        But you are gentle
        And you are kind.
        That's why I love you
        Ten times more,
        So please don't ask me
        Questions anymore."

But the orca, as you can see,
Still continued to disagree,
A pain in the neck, goodness me,
Don't you agree?

The now crying orca
In confusion further asked,
"How can you love me
When you can't be with me?"

The panda replied, this time teary-eyed,
"But love knows no reason
And has no boundaries like time."
"I'm still here, can't you see?
Because I wouldn't trade you
For anything in the world,
Not even for my carrot food.
And I won't force you to eat
Bamboo grass, I promise."

"We are different, that, I get,
We're both unique in our own way,
But we're also the same, don't you realize?
We're both made of black and white."
"I just love you immensely,

You make me so happy
Even if happiness means
Loving you from afar
Under the aurora skies
Full of bright stars."


"I love you, too",
Said the orca to the panda,
No questions asked,
Just a love to forever last.

# *The Sun and the Sunflower*

For years, the sunflower
        Has always asked
        The summer sun
To never leave her side;
And the sun
Has always calmly replied,
"I won't leave.
I will never let you out of my sight".

But one day,
    The sweet sunflower
    Got scared,
    As one of her petals
    Fell on the ground.

In fear to be seen
    While fading, sensing
    The immense emptiness
    Edging closer to despair,
    She asked the sun
    To leave her instead;
    Broken
    And torn deep inside,
    She pretended not to care.


And in that moment
    It started to rain
    After the sun rapidly descended,
    Hurriedly leaving his only flower,
    Not knowing her deep love,
    Unuttered.


Suddenly the rain
    Forgivingly stopped,
    But the unforgotten pain never did,
    And in her darkest hour,
    A star appeared.


With whispered apologies,
    She silently wished he had stayed,
    Not believing her wounding lie
    When she asked him to go away.

So in her unshed tears
    Of unspoken regrets
    ... She said goodbye,
    But the little star,
    The sun in disguise replied,
    "I never left."
    "I'm here, don't ever forget".

# Home

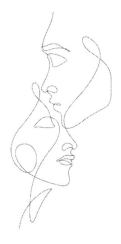

# My Home Is You

If home is a place
Where words hold me,
And every line creates
Such a sweet melody...

If home is a sanctuary,
So serene and sacred
Where I could just be me,
Loved and accepted—

Then my home is you.

# Love Forgives

Only love forgives—
It soothes the heart of anger
Like soft falling rain.

# Bleed

I have willed
    To forgive
        What made me bleed.

# While Flowers Wait

What awaits me in the afterlife?
Will my faith be enough?
Will I find peace and wholeness
In the midst of endless chaos?
Will love find me when I can't find myself?
Will hope hold me when I'm about to give up?
Will courage prevail in moments that I fail?
Will faith sustain me and fill my sails when I'm too frail?
Will truth be my guiding light
In my dreary days and empty nights?
Will I abide daily in kindness
And stand faithfully to reject what's worldly?
Will I remain anchored in grace
As I strive to be worthy and see the light of glory?
This is my desire in the silence of my heart,
For my soul to persevere until the last
And meet my Creator one day
In a place where there will be no more tears of pain.

In the meantime, while flowers wait
    For sunshine and rain
    And I face the harsh realities of life—
    I live to glorify His name.

## The Gift

L et's unwrap the gift
Of life's little surprises
With a childlike heart.

# Faith's Fragrance

L ittle white jasmine
Like clouds' sweet silver lining
And pearl scents of faith.

# When You Find Me

I crave darkness, sometimes.

It's the first thought that comes to mind as I settle myself in the little corner of my room, lights off, and I close my eyes, as if there's still no enough darkness.

And I ask myself why is it so fulfilling to be like this. Then I realize, it's not the darkness that I crave really.

It's the nothingness because I can't see anything.

It's the stillness it brings me.

It's the quiet night.

It's the space that I feel.

It's the silence of my heart.

It's the peace inside my head.

It's the free will to stay or leave.

It's the assurance that I have a choice.

It's the readiness to choose what I desire.

It's the grace that reminds me that I am whole.

It's the hope that once I press the switch on, you'd find me.

I crave darkness, sometimes...

　　because it is only in darkness that you can shine on me and I become everything— the shadow that delights in being found in the light of your love.


And when you find me, when your hand reaches for mine, I know I'll find the most cherished thing my soul loves.

# Echo

May silence
Never echo goodbye,
For flowers,
Too, cry
While we are
Aching to speak.

# All My Tomorrows

I may not say
    "I love you" now,
        But I know
That I want you
To be part of
All my tomorrows.

# Clouds

This world
     Made me cold,
     You gave me
A song and
Touched my soul.

My heart
     Was made of stone,
     You brought me
     To tears and
     Made me feel.

The walls
     I had built for so long
     Broke down
     Unexpectedly
     When you came along.

At dawn,
    We will be clouds,
    Dancing in the sunlight,
    You and I,
    No matter what.

# Retrace

L et love lace
   Our lives with grace
   As we retrace steps
Without regrets.

# Bloom

When a bud opens up,
　　Let her bloom
　　And let her show you how
　　She made it through the storm.

## *Loved*

Would you love her
Just the same
If you knew?
She bleeds words,
Holding stars
In subtle metaphors
Your heart can't ignore,
And when she loves
No one but you,
Forever in her lines,
And simple rhymes,
You'll find yourself
Loved, too.

# Between Always and Goodbye

She's not a queen
Of smiles and sighs,
She's not a princess
Who lets her heart decide,
But if the road will lead
Her back to you
Without disguise,
The moon will know
Her name,
And the stars
Will never be lost again
Between always
And goodbye.

# The Summer It Rained

C ompletely unguarded,
     I felt the cold, harsh wind
        Sending shivers down my spine,
Despair seeping through
My leaking heart
And aching mind.


It then started raining
    That one summer night.


My laughter faded
    When cold, fine drops
    Subtly fell on my face.
    But somehow,
    It felt good inside
    To let the freezing drizzle
    Touch my skin, kiss my lips.
    Little salty droplets,
    They tasted just like my tears
    Of unfeigned feelings
    And broken rhymes.

Then you found me.
    How can I not love you?


You painted me with the colors
    Of red, orange, and yellow
    And splashed hues of
    Green, blue and indigo.
    You painted rainbows in my sky
    When, in the twilight,
    I was lost—
    The summer it rained.

# Three Words

I might say the words
    I long to tell you, one day soon.
    And when I do, you'll know
I'll forever hold you
And I will never let go.

# *Stillness*

And when stillness
Finally meets
The unforgiving chaos,
Each breath of silence
Says so much more.

# Unspoken Poem

You're the poem,
Unspoken;
I'll find you
In every eclipse
And hold you
In my dreams,
As shadows
Fall on pages
Of a script,
Hoping words
Would soothe
And decrypt.

# Sunshine in Our Pain

When we learn the grace to soften
All these dark parts of life we've seen,
We will hope through the noise,
No matter how much it hurts,
For the skeletons in our closets
Need be conquered, not hidden,
As we find sunshine in our pain,
A quiet place in the pelting rain,
And though we'll ache as we embrace
This new light in each other's darkness,
Love will fill the emptiness in our hearts,
Knowing that nothing can keep us apart.

L ove is
Waking up to be hugged
By every poem that makes me feel loved.

Love is
One hug from you each day,
Consistently, without fail.

Love is
Writing letters to each other,
Rhyming lines that bring us closer.

Love is
Spending time together without pretense,
Knowing that we are seen, heard and held.

Love is
Holding space for myself to reflect
And to explore my feelings as I learn to accept.

Love is
Having misunderstandings until it pains,
But never walking away even if it rains.

Love is
Saying sorry for every mistake
And making amends whatever it takes.

Love is
Forgiving despite the what and why,
Without the need to say goodbye.

Love is
Still choosing us after all the upsets,
Before we sleep, before the sun sets.

Love is
Having no reason why I love you,
But knowing what love means because of you.

# Unravel

May joy's gentle wind
Unravel today
The love we held
In our poems yesterday.

# It's Love

You know it's love
When you prayed to heavens above,
In supplication, on bended knees,
"I love him, Lord, protect him, please".

# All I Need

How do I quiet my heart
From all that I feel inside?
How do I heal from the hurt
As I ease my mind?
How do I love just enough
To take risk completely?
How do I let you know?
All I need is your faith in me.

# The Missing Piece of Me

May the stars shine softly
        While I feel you in each poem,
        Layers of love, hope, and glee,
Gently tucked in the evening's gloam,
Finding in you the missing piece of me
As we dance in our dreams and freely roam,
Waiting to be hugged by the sweetest poetry,
Reminding me, once again, why I am your home.

# When Words Fail You

When words fail you,
When sadness comforts your fears
And your smile is replaced with tears,
I will still be here, holding your hand,
Assuring you that my faith and love
Will always be more than enough
To carry us through no matter what,
Even more so, when life gets tough.

When words fail you,
I will patiently wait, I will stay true,
And I will love you constantly more
When, in darkness, silence roars,
Until the stars hug me again,
Until your hand firmly holds mine again,
Never letting go in times of trouble:
I'll stand by you through it all.

And when your words find me again,
I will know that I am back home,
With confidence and hope regained,
It's all I ever want for all my days.
I know I would never ask for more
Than just to be held in your loving arms
As we wake up to the dawn's soft light,
And bask in the gentlest gloam of night.

# Petals

⌒⌒⌒

The space between
    Petals of love and ache
    Mirrors the distance
Between us—
Comforted by faith.

## Joy

Each breath of joy
    Nestles in warm hugs
    And tender kisses
When pleasure delights
The untamable passion.

# The Brightest

I wrote letters to the stone,
To the sun and to the moon,
I wished fireflies and clouds
Wouldn't fade away too soon,
I dreamed through the scream
Of the haunting melancholy,
And then I found love when
You did find your way to me,
For you are my soul's desire,
And the keeper of my heart,
You're the rhyme in my lines,
The brightest of all the stars.

# Safe Arms

And when distance
      Comes between us,
        Remind me again
That you love me,
Until I am wrapped
In your safe arms,
Where you'd finally
Hold me so tightly,
And kiss me, longer
Than I've imagined;
Tell me once more
That you are mine.

# After the Rain

Your heart breaks,
    For your dreams are as shattered as hers,
    The remnants of a song
In desolate quietness give no remedy,
Leaving her so loved yet so broken,
Hidden from you, unknown to many.
But as the gleaming city lights
Chased the night
When her only choice was to be unseen,
Almost drifting to oblivion,
You saw a different her.


Yours is a delicate love
    While the scent of dawn seems elusive,
    And the unswerving melancholy
    Taints her dearest memory;
    You patiently wait for the wind
    To play with her hair.

"Trust the universe", you said to her,
    For she's your moon now,
    Drenched in all her stars,
    But tomorrow she'll be sun,
    Cloaked in rays of brilliance.


And one day soon, she will be there—
    A rosette of charming simplicity
    Basking in your warmth
    After the rain.

# Traces

Hope will find me
Where faith
Left traces of your love.

# Remedy

Your words love me.
  Your love heals me—
  My soul's remedy.

# Time

Time will always have
Fond memories of us,
How we truly care,
How we trust,
Though the shards
Of the present remain,
And the same scars
Have yet to fade—
We still love.


And in between
The coldest nights
And city lights,
You hide me
Deep within your lines,
And I hold you,
Deep in my heart.

Under different skies,
   We rest in uncertainty
   And we accept love
   In its pure simplicity.

# Whole

If I must break,
  Let me break like
  The falling rain—
Let tears make
The flowers glisten,
As clock ticks and
Love softly speaks
Of its truest emotions,
Between here and there
Where silence sits still,
While time and space
Pretend to never care.

For if I must break,
    I must have truly loved.
    So let me tell you honestly
    All that I wanted to say
    And let me find my way,
    Let me stubbornly love,
    Let me give it all.


Let me love and be loved,
    And let it make me whole.

# Jasmine

They called me rain,
  And then they called me summer,
  But now,
For you,
I am the flower
That breathes your name.

# About the Author

Jasmine Miró is an accountant by profession and a poet by choice. Born into a family that is deeply rooted in business and finance, with both parents and siblings dedicated to the field, Jasmine was trained to control her emotions and maintain a tough exterior. Her degree in accounting and her expertise in finance and supply chain reflect this disciplined upbringing.

However, outside of her professional life, Jasmine turns to poetry as a means of self-expression. For her, writing poetry is a tool to explore and articulate her innermost thoughts and feelings. She believes that true understanding of oneself and others is best achieved through the written word. By capturing her emotions in poetry and then revisiting them as an observer, she gains a fresh perspective, allowing her to see with a different set of eyes.

Made in the USA
Columbia, SC
13 August 2024